BEST OF THE SUPER BOWL

GREAT SUPER BOWL DYNASTIES

BY DAVID J. CLARKE

SportsZone

An Imprint of Abdo Publishing
abdobooks.com

abdobooks.com

Printed in the United States of America, North Mankato, Minnesota.
102024
012025

THIS BOOK CONTAINS RECYCLED MATERIALS

Cover Photos: Focus On Sport/Getty Images (left); Tim Warner/Getty Images Sport/Getty Images (middle); Rob Brown/Getty Images Sport/Getty Images (right)
Interior Photos: Tony Tomsic/AP Images, 4, 13; James Flores/Getty Images Sport/Getty Images, 6; Focus On Sport/Getty Images Sport/Getty Images, 8, 27, 44; George Gojkovich/Getty Images Sport/Getty Images, 10; Al Messerschmidt/AP Images, 14; Focus On Sport/Getty Images, 16; Peter Read Miller/AP Images, 18; Bettmann/Getty Images, 20; Rich Pilling/Sporting News Archive/Getty Images, 22; Tim Sharp/AP Images, 25; Albert Dickson/Sporting News Archive/Getty Images, 29; Sporting News/Getty Images, 30; Nancy Kerrigan/Getty Images Sport/Getty Images, 32; Timothy A. Clary/AFP/Getty Images, 34, 45; Ric Tapia/AP Images, 35; Rich Graessle/Icon Sportswire/Getty Images, 37; Patrick Smith/Getty Images Sport/Getty Images, 38; Matthew Stockman/Getty Images Sport/Getty Images, 40; Michael Reaves/Getty Images Sport/Getty Images, 43

Editor: Charlie Beattie
Series Designer: Jake Slavik

Library of Congress Control Number: 2024938392

Publisher's Cataloging-in-Publication Data

Names: Clarke, David J., author.
Title: Great Super Bowl dynasties / by David J. Clarke
Description: Minneapolis, Minnesota: ABDO Publishing, 2025 | Series: Best of the Super Bowl | Includes online resources and index.
Identifiers: ISBN 9781098295417 (lib. bdg.) | ISBN 9798384916413 (ebook)
Subjects: LCSH: Super Bowl--Records--Juvenile literature. | Football teams--Juvenile literature. | American football--Juvenile literature. | National Football League--Juvenile literature. | Super Bowl champions--Juvenile literature. | Football--United States--History--Juvenile literature.
Classification: DDC 796.332648--dc23

TABLE OF CONTENTS

CHAPTER ONE

THE FIRST DYNASTY

In the summer of 1959, the Green Bay Packers were looking for a new coach. The team had a glorious past in the National Football League (NFL). But the Packers had been struggling for more than a decade.

They chose an assistant from the New York Giants named Vince Lombardi. Not many fans knew who he was. The hire turned out to be the best thing that ever happened to the Packers.

Lombardi was a tough, disciplined head coach. One of his famous quotes was, "Winning is not a sometime thing. It's an all-time thing." To play for Lombardi's Packers, a player had to do the right thing on every play. It was hard work. But his players loved him. They also loved that he won games. The Packers had won just one of 12 games

Vince Lombardi compiled a 96-34-6 record in nine seasons with the Green Bay Packers. He was also 9-1 in postseason games.

Green Bay running back Elijah Pitts (22) runs behind lineman Jerry Kramer (64) in Super Bowl I on January 15, 1967.

in 1958. In 1959, the team went 7–5. In 1961, the Packers won the first of back-to-back NFL championships.

Around that same time, the American Football League (AFL) was forming. For a half decade, the NFL and the AFL fought over the best players. But the leagues never met on the field.

Everything changed in June 1966. That year, the leagues decided to merge. In 1970, the AFL teams would officially join the NFL. Until then, the two league champions would meet in an annual title game. The first one was played on January 15, 1967. It was called the AFL-NFL World Championship Game. Within a few years it would have a new name—the Super Bowl.

PACKER SWEEP

The Kansas City Chiefs represented the AFL in the first Super Bowl. Waiting for them in the Los Angeles Coliseum were the mighty Packers. Green Bay was already known as the top team in either league. The Packers had also won the previous year's NFL title in 1965.

Coming into Super Bowl I, the Packers boasted talent on both sides of the ball. In 1966, the Packers' defense was spectacular. The group held opponents to 11.6 points per game. That excellent defense was backed by a fearsome running game. The Packers' most famous play was the power sweep. Quarterback Bart Starr would toss to a running back who was running wide. Linemen would hop out of their stances and race in front of the back, forming a wall of blockers. Green Bay ran it so well that it became known as the "Packer Sweep." Both units thrived in Super Bowl I. The Packers' defense held the Chiefs to 10 points.

HALL OF FAME TALENTS

In addition to coach Vince Lombardi, 11 players who appeared for the Packers in the first two Super Bowls are in the Hall of Fame. Quarterback Bart Starr led the offense. He was joined by running backs Jim Taylor and Paul Hornung. Linemen Jerry Kramer and Forrest Gregg are also enshrined. Hall of Fame defensive players included linemen Henry Jordan and Willie Davis, linebackers Ray Nitschke and Dave Robinson, and defensive backs Herb Adderley and Willie Wood.

Meanwhile, the offense ran for 130 yards and three touchdowns in a 35–10 victory.

FOR ALL TIME

Lombardi was considered one of the NFL's great coaches even before the Packers won Super Bowl I. And though the Packers were an aging team in 1967, Lombardi guided Green Bay to another Super Bowl. Before the game, rumors were swirling that it might be the 54-year-old's last game with the team.

Quarterback Bart Starr was named the Most Valuable Player (MVP) of both Super Bowl I and Super Bowl II.

Green Bay squared off against the Oakland Raiders in what is now known as Super Bowl II. The Raiders had an excellent passing attack, led by strong-armed quarterback Daryle Lamonica. But it was the Packers who went deep early in the game. Less than four minutes into the second quarter, Starr drilled a 62-yard touchdown pass to star receiver Boyd Dowler. The score helped Green Bay build a 16–7 halftime lead.

Despite the advantage, the Packers felt like they had been sloppy. It was not the kind of football their beloved head coach wanted. If it was going to be Lombardi's last game, the players wanted to send him out the right way. As one Packer put it, the team decided to play the second half "for the old man."

The team led 26–7 in the fourth quarter when cornerback Herb Adderley put the finishing touch on the win. He picked off a Lamonica pass and raced 60 yards for a touchdown. After the game, offensive linemen Forrest Gregg and Jerry Kramer carried Lombardi off the field.

Lombardi did retire from coaching the Packers after the game. Two years later, the NFL legend passed away. The league decided to honor Lombardi by naming the Super Bowl trophy after him. To this day, any team that wins a Super Bowl feels the legacy of the game's first dynasty in their hands.

12
Pittsburgh Steelers Coach

CHAPTER TWO

THE STEEL CURTAIN

The Pittsburgh Steelers were founded in 1933. Entering the 1970s, the team had done a lot of losing. Pittsburgh had a winning record only seven times in its first 37 seasons. And the Steelers had never won a playoff game.

However, Pittsburgh made a smart coaching hire in January 1969. Chuck Noll had been the defensive coordinator for the Baltimore Colts, who had reached that year's Super Bowl. Noll was a quiet, private man who was known as a great teacher.

The team also made smart draft picks. In 1969, Pittsburgh picked defensive lineman "Mean" Joe Greene in the first round. A year later, the Steelers selected strong-armed quarterback Terry Bradshaw first overall. In 1971, linebacker Jack Ham was the team's top choice. All three players eventually reached the Pro Football Hall of Fame.

Chuck Noll, *right*, coached the Steelers from 1969 to 1991.

The players Pittsburgh selected all had one thing in common. They were all incredibly tough. That fit the city they played in. Pittsburgh is known as the "Steel City." The blue-collar workers who went to Steelers games loved their new, hard-nosed team.

THE CLASS OF '74

The Steelers drafted well in the early 1970s. But the team's best class came along in 1974. Pittsburgh took graceful wide receiver Lynn Swann in the first round. Terrifying linebacker Jack Lambert was the Steelers' second-round pick. Receiver John Stallworth went in the third round. Finally, center "Iron" Mike Webster was taken in the fifth round. All four players eventually wound up in the Pro Football Hall of Fame.

REACHING THE TOP

Pittsburgh improved slowly. The Steelers won their first playoff game in 1972. But the American Football Conference (AFC) was filled with tough teams such as the Miami Dolphins and the Oakland Raiders. It took until the 1974 season for Pittsburgh to break through to the Super Bowl.

The Steelers' fierce defense led the way. Greene, Ham, defensive end L. C. Greenwood, and linebackers Jack Lambert and Andy Russell led a stout unit. It was nicknamed the "Steel Curtain." Cornerback Mel Blount and safety Mike Wagner held things down in the secondary. However, Pittsburgh faced another tough defense in Super Bowl IX on January 12, 1975. Behind the

The fearsome Steelers defense held Minnesota to a Super Bowl–low 119 yards in Super Bowl IX after the 1974 season.

"Purple People Eaters" defensive line, the Minnesota Vikings held the Steelers to 16 points. But Pittsburgh's defense proved superior in a 16–6 win. Two of Pittsburgh's points came on the Super Bowl's first safety. Lineman Dwight White sacked Minnesota quarterback Fran Tarkenton in the end zone in the second quarter.

Pittsburgh was suddenly a championship town. And the Steelers proved it was no fluke a year later. Bradshaw and wide receiver Lynn Swann hooked up on a few highlight-reel passes. But it was the defense that stepped up in the end against the Dallas Cowboys.

Pittsburgh running back Franco Harris (32) looks for an opening in Super Bowl XIII on January 21, 1979, against the Dallas Cowboys.

Safety Glen Edwards picked off a Dallas pass in Super Bowl X's final seconds to preserve a 21–17 victory.

AIRING IT OUT

The Steelers missed out on the next two championship tilts. But the team was back in a big way in 1978. By that season, Pittsburgh's offense was the key to the team. Bradshaw was the NFL's MVP. Swann formed a potent combination with fellow receiver John Stallworth. In the backfield, tough running backs Franco Harris and Rocky Bleier worked behind a physical offensive line.

The Steelers needed that firepower in Super Bowl XIII. The game was a rematch with the Cowboys. Bradshaw and Dallas quarterback Roger Staubach both had incredible passing days. The teams combined for 687 yards of offense. After a back-and-forth first half, Pittsburgh took a 21–17 lead into the fourth quarter.

With just over seven minutes to go, Harris sprinted in for a 22-yard touchdown run. Dallas then fumbled the kickoff, and the Steelers recovered at the Cowboys' 18. On the next play, Bradshaw lofted a pass to Swann. The star receiver made a fingertip grab in the end zone. After the extra point, Pittsburgh had a 35–17 lead. Dallas rallied by scoring two touchdowns late in the game. But Pittsburgh held on for a thrilling 35–31 win. Bradshaw was named the game's MVP. The Steelers were the first team to ever win the Super Bowl three times. And they weren't done yet.

Pittsburgh receiver John Stallworth races for the winning touchdown in Super Bowl XIV after the 1979 season.

No offense scored more points than the Steelers in 1979. Pittsburgh streaked to a 12–4 regular season record. The Steelers then rolled through the playoffs and into Super Bowl XIV against the Los Angeles Rams.

Once again, the game was close. But the Steelers showed their toughness in the fourth quarter. With just over 12 minutes to play and trailing 19–17, Pittsburgh had the ball at its own 27. Bradshaw heaved a deep pass looking for Stallworth. A Rams' defensive back leaped to swat it away but missed. Stallworth hauled in the pass and raced untouched to the end zone. A 1-yard touchdown run from Harris with 1:52 left sealed the 31–19 victory.

The NFL was filled with excellent teams in the 1970s. It is considered one of the most competitive decades the league has ever seen. In addition to Pittsburgh, Dallas and Miami both won multiple Super Bowls. An excellent Oakland team won only once. Other star-powered teams like the Vikings didn't win a single championship. But Pittsburgh left no doubt as to who was the decade's best. The Steelers entered the 1970s as one of the NFL's worst teams. They finished as the most successful franchise of the Super Bowl era.

BIKE
16
16

CHAPTER THREE

DYNASTY RIVALS

As the 1980s dawned, the Pittsburgh Steelers stood atop the football world. But another surprising team was about to take Pittsburgh's place. The San Francisco 49ers had suffered through seven losing seasons in eight years entering 1981. But the team had an innovative head coach in Bill Walsh.

In the 1970s, most NFL teams either ran the ball or threw deep passes. Walsh designed an offense that would move the ball with quick, short throws. That way, teams couldn't get to his quarterback in time to sack him. It became known as the West Coast offense.

To run it, Walsh drafted Joe Montana out of Notre Dame in 1979. Montana didn't have a rocket arm. But he was calm, smart, and accurate. In 1981, he led San Francisco to a 13–3 record. After beating the Dallas Cowboys on a last-second touchdown in the National

Joe Montana was the NFL's regular season MVP twice and won the Super Bowl MVP Award three times.

Football Conference (NFC) title game, San Francisco earned a spot in Super Bowl XVI.

The 49ers jumped out to a 20–0 halftime lead over the Cincinnati Bengals. But the Bengals charged back. Only a key goal-line stand in the third quarter kept the score 20–7. San Francisco's defense stopped four Cincinnati plays from inside the 2-yard line. In the end, the 49ers won 26–21 to claim their first title.

Bill Walsh's revolutionary offensive game plans changed the NFL in the 1980s.

AIR ATTACK

Walsh's offense helped turn the NFL into a passing league. Throughout the 1984 season, the 49ers used the West Coast offense to finish 15–1 and reach the Super Bowl again. Montana and dual-threat running back Roger Craig led the way. But San Francisco was facing a stellar quarterback on the other side. The Miami Dolphins' Dan Marino had thrown for NFL records of 5,084 yards and 48 touchdowns.

Montana upstaged his fellow Hall of Fame quarterback at Super Bowl XIX. The game was in Palo Alto, California, just south of San Francisco. Montana felt right at home throwing for a Super Bowl–record 331 yards and three touchdowns. Craig caught two of them. He also ran for a score to become the first NFL player to record three touchdowns in one Super Bowl. The 49ers romped 38–16.

BACK-TO-BACK

The summer after winning Super Bowl XIX, San Francisco added a young wide receiver in the NFL Draft named Jerry Rice. Rice would go on to become the best at his position. Yet despite their many weapons, the 49ers didn't reach the Super Bowl again until after the 1988 season.

In his final year as head coach, Walsh admitted he didn't think it was San Francisco's best team. The 49ers finished 10–6. But the team managed to reach Super Bowl XXIII for a rematch with the Bengals.

San Francisco wide receiver Jerry Rice breaks a tackle after making one of his 11 receptions in Super Bowl XXIII on January 22, 1989.

The game was close throughout. San Francisco trailed 16–13 late in the fourth quarter. Even worse, the 49ers were backed up to their own 8-yard line. But Montana had a reputation for being calm under pressure. "Joe Cool" guided the team on a 92-yard drive. He capped it off by hitting receiver John Taylor on a 10-yard strike with 32 seconds left to deliver a third title.

With the retirement of Walsh, George Seifert took over as San Francisco's coach. Other than that, little changed in the 1989 season. The 49ers finished 14–2. In the postseason, they outscored their opponents 126–26.

The finishing touch was a masterful performance against the Denver Broncos in Super Bowl XXIV. Montana found Rice for a 20-yard touchdown pass just 4:22 into the game. That fast start helped the 49ers build a 27–3 halftime lead. By the time it was over, the pair had connected twice more. The game was the biggest blowout in Super Bowl history. San Francisco ran away with a 55–10 win.

NFC DYNASTY

San Francisco's win over the Miami Dolphins in Super Bowl XIX started a streak by NFC teams. The conference won 13 straight Super Bowls. And the games were rarely close. The average victory margin was 19.9 points per game. Only two of the 13 games were decided by a touchdown or less. The Denver Broncos finally broke the string by beating the Green Bay Packers 31–24 in Super Bowl XXXII on January 25, 1998.

DALLAS REVIVAL

As the 49ers were becoming the team of the 1980s, the Cowboys were sinking. Dallas had reached five Super Bowls in the 1970s, winning two. Along the way, the popular Cowboys had been dubbed "America's Team." But in 1989, Dallas finished 1–15. That proved to be the low point for the franchise. However, a new owner and coach were about to turn things around.

Billionaire Jerry Jones bought the Cowboys that year. One of his first moves was to fire legendary head coach Tom Landry and replace him with Jimmy Johnson. The team also started adding young talent in the draft. Between 1988 and 1990, Dallas took wide receiver Michael Irvin, quarterback Troy Aikman, and running back Emmitt Smith, all in the first round. The three players would become known as the "Triplets."

They also helped lead Dallas back to glory. By 1992, the Cowboys were a winning team full of confidence. They weren't much like the humble, beloved Cowboys of the 1970s. The 1990s teams were full of trash-talkers. Opposing fans hated them. Dallas fans didn't care.

In January 1993, the Cowboys beat San Francisco 30–20 to reach Super Bowl XXVII. The win sent Dallas back to the Super Bowl for the first time since the 1977 season. It also started a rivalry between the two dominant NFC teams of the early 1990s.

The Cowboys finished off the championship run by routing the Buffalo Bills 52–17. Aikman threw four touchdown passes. Two of

From left, Troy Aikman, Emmitt Smith, and Michael Irvin were the key offensive players for the Dallas Cowboys dynasty of the 1990s.

them went to Irvin. The Cowboys defense forced a Super Bowl–record nine turnovers.

EMMITT'S BIG DAY

Dallas raced through the 1993 season at 12–4. A big reason why was Smith, who was named the league's MVP. In the NFC title game against San Francisco, he ran for a touchdown and caught another. That set up a Super Bowl rematch with Buffalo.

The game was tied 13–13 in the third quarter. The Cowboys got the ball and drove 64 yards for the go-ahead score. Smith carried the ball on seven of the drive's eight plays. He finished it off with a 15-yard scamper to the end zone. Dallas went on to repeat as champions with a 30–13 win.

YOUNG'S MOMENT

By the start of the 1994 season, Dallas and San Francisco were the top attractions in the NFL. But things had changed for both. Jones and Johnson had argued over who should get credit for Dallas's rise. Ultimately Jones fired Johnson and hired Barry Switzer instead.

San Francisco's big change had come earlier. After the 1992 season, the 49ers traded Montana to the Kansas City Chiefs. His longtime backup, Steve Young, took over. But after San Francisco lost back-to-back NFC title games to the Cowboys, 49ers fans wondered if Young had what it took to be a champion.

He answered his critics in that 1994 season. Young was named the NFL's MVP. He then threw two touchdown passes and scrambled for another in a 38–28 NFC title game win over Dallas. That set up a sweet performance in the Super Bowl. Facing the overmatched San Diego Chargers, Young aired it out early and often. He tossed a 44-yard touchdown pass to Rice on the game's third play. By the time the 49–26 beating was over, Young had thrown a Super Bowl–record six scores. The 49ers' fifth Super Bowl win was also the most ever.

Steve Young, *right*, celebrates with Jerry Rice after the pair connected on a touchdown pass during Super Bowl XXXIX in January 1995.

DALLAS DEFENSE

Free agency had been new to the NFL in 1992. The Cowboys were the first team to spend big on new players. That summer, Dallas had thrown big money at future Hall of Fame defensive end Charles Haley. The former 49er had helped the Cowboys defense become a sturdy group.

After losing the NFL title game to San Francisco in 1994, Dallas swiped Deion Sanders from the 49ers. Sanders was such an intimidating force that few quarterbacks even tried to throw his way. And he helped tip the NFC back in Dallas's favor.

In January 1996, the star-studded Cowboys were back in the Super Bowl. Their opponents were the Pittsburgh Steelers, who had beaten Dallas twice in championship matchups during the 1970s. Whoever won this time would join San Francisco as five-time Super Bowl winners.

In a tight game, the Steelers avoided Sanders. In fact, "Neon Deion's" biggest play was a 47-yard reception in the first half when he lined up at wide receiver. Instead, Steelers quarterback Neil O'Donnell spent the game trying to throw against Dallas's other cornerback, Larry Brown. The plan backfired when Brown intercepted O'Donnell twice in the second half. Both picks led to Dallas scores in a 27–17 victory.

The win ended the dominant run for both teams. San Francisco didn't reach another Super Bowl until the 2011 season. More than a decade after that, Dallas was still searching for its next trip to the big game. And still neither team had won another championship. But the teams' overlapping dynasties provided some of the Super Bowl's most memorable winners.

Larry Brown had six interceptions during the 1995 regular season and three more in the playoffs.

MOTOROLA

CHAPTER FOUR

THE PATRIOT WAY

Some Super Bowl dynasties have been spread out over multiple years. Others feature a cluster of wins in a span of four or five seasons. The New England Patriots of the 2000s were both. But at the beginning, no one saw it coming.

By 2001, the New England Patriots had been around for 41 years. The team spent 10 championship-less seasons in the AFL. The losing ways mostly continued after the 1970 merger. New England's high points came in losing the Super Bowls after the 1985 and 1995 seasons.

No one was expecting much of the Patriots going into the 2001 season. New England had finished 5–11 the year before. Things seemed worse in September when star quarterback Drew Bledsoe was knocked out with an injury in the team's second game of

Hiring Bill Belichick as head coach in 2000 helped turn the New England Patriots into a powerhouse franchise.

Adam Vinatieri connects on his game-winning 48-yard field goal in Super Bowl XXXVI on February 3, 2002.

the season. In Bledsoe's place came unknown second-year backup Tom Brady. That's how one of football's greatest dynasties began.

Brady's steady play that season led New England all the way to Super Bowl XXXVI. But most thought the fairy tale would end there. The Patriots were big underdogs against the St. Louis Rams, who had won the title two years earlier and boasted an incredible offense. However, the Patriots head coach was Bill Belichick, who was known as a master of defensive game plans. He shut down the Rams. With just minutes to play, the game was deadlocked 17–17. Brady guided

New England's offense down the field. Kicker Adam Vinatieri drilled the game-winning 48-yard field goal as time ran out. The Patriots were champions for the first time.

After missing the playoffs a year later, the Patriots bounced back in 2003. The team finished 14–2 and reached Super Bowl XXXVIII against the Carolina Panthers. Once again, the game came down to a late field goal by Vinatieri. With nine seconds left, his 41-yard boot delivered another title.

SUCCESS AND SCANDAL

By the time the Patriots faced the Philadelphia Eagles in Super Bowl XXXIX on February 6, 2005, New England had a reputation. Belichick was now thought of as the NFL's smartest head coach. Brady was the quarterback who never seemed to lose. Few other Patriots were considered big stars, but the team always seemed to have the right player in the right spot every game.

That was true again in another tight Super Bowl game. Brady threw two touchdown passes. For the second straight year, one of them went to a linebacker named Mike Vrabel, who had lined up as a tight end on the play. In the end, New England pulled out a 24–21 win.

Despite being viewed as the NFL's premier team, the Patriots didn't reach the Super Bowl again until 2008. That year, they were back with a vengeance. New England entered the game 18–0.

Only the 1972 Miami Dolphins had ever finished an NFL season with a perfect record. But those Dolphins only needed 17 games to finish as champions. A 19–0 season would surely make New England the greatest team ever.

However, the underdog New York Giants shocked New England in Super Bowl XLII to win 17–14. And that was just the start of New England's problems. All season, the NFL had been investigating the Patriots for spying on other team's practices with hidden

Tom Brady was the only player to appear in all six of New England's Super Bowl victories in the 2000s and 2010s.

video cameras. Reports showed that New England had been doing it since their first Super Bowl win in 2002. Some argued that the Patriots should forfeit some of their championship trophies. In the end, that did not happen. But the Patriots' success was tainted in the eyes of many NFL observers by the scandal known as "Spygate."

DEFLATEGATE

After the 2015 AFC title game, the NFL tested the footballs used by Tom Brady in New England's win over the Indianapolis Colts. The league found that the balls weren't inflated as much as they should be, and that Brady knew about it. In the end, Brady was suspended four games to start the 2016 season. The scandal became known as "Deflategate."

DYNASTY PART TWO

The Patriots remained contenders throughout everything. They reached another Super Bowl after the 2011 season but were upset by the Giants again. Still, New England was the NFL's most feared team each year. In 2014, the Patriots once again were AFC champions. That set up a matchup with the Seattle Seahawks in Super Bowl XLIX on February 1, 2015.

As with the Patriots' five previous Super Bowls under Belichick, the game was close. Brady threw two fourth-quarter touchdown passes to rally for a 28–24 lead. That held up when backup cornerback Malcolm Butler picked off a Seattle pass at the goal line in the game's final minute.

That comeback was thrilling, but it was nothing compared to Super Bowl LI after the 2016 season. Facing the Atlanta Falcons, the Patriots stumbled through the first half and found themselves down 28–3 early in the third quarter. No NFL team had ever rallied from more than 10 points down in a Super Bowl. But throughout the team's run of dominance, Brady and the Patriots had seemingly always found a way to win. Brady threw two touchdown passes as New England clawed back. Running back James White tied the score 28–28 on a 1-yard touchdown run with 57 seconds left. New England got the ball to start overtime and went 75 yards in less than four minutes. White capped off the incredible comeback with a two-yard plunge and a fifth title.

The Patriots reached the Super Bowl again a year later but lost a 41–33 shoot-out to the Eagles. Fans had started to wonder if that was the end of New England's run. Brady was now 41 years old. In addition, he and Belichick didn't always see eye-to-eye anymore.

However, New England put together one final run to Super Bowl LIII. This time the matchup was with the Los Angeles Rams, who featured a spectacular wide-open passing offense. Belichick showed he still had a knack for defensive game-planning. The Patriots stuffed the Rams in a 13–3 victory.

The Patriots' dynasty ended after a playoff loss in 2019. But the legacy left behind was amazing. Over a span of 18 seasons, New England reached nine Super Bowls and won six.

The Patriots' 34–28 victory over the Atlanta Falcons in Super Bowl LI was the first Super Bowl decided in overtime.

15
LIV

CHAPTER FIVE

KINGS IN KANSAS CITY

Most NFL dynasties begin when a team finds the right quarterback. That was true for the Kansas City Chiefs. The team traded up in the 2017 draft to select a prolific passer from Texas Tech named Patrick Mahomes.

The Chiefs had played in two of the first four Super Bowls. In January 1970, they defeated the Minnesota Vikings to win Super Bowl IV. Then the playoffs became a nightmare. Over the next 49 seasons, Kansas City won just four postseason games. But with the addition of Mahomes, the pieces were falling into place.

Mahomes brought excitement on every play with his rocket arm and ability to make highlight-reel throws. He also had speedy wide receivers such as Tyreek Hill to throw to and one of the game's top

After spending his rookie season as a backup, Patrick Mahomes quickly became one of the top quarterbacks in the NFL.

tight ends in Travis Kelce. Running the show was Andy Reid. The burly, likeable head coach was known as an offensive genius.

Things came together for Kansas City after the 2019 season. The Chiefs finished 12–4 and reached Super Bowl LIV against the San Francisco 49ers. Early in the fourth quarter, the Chiefs' high-powered offense was stuck. They trailed the 49ers 20–10. It was then that Mahomes showed his incredible big-game skills. He threw two

Kansas City coach Andy Reid had won more than 200 NFL games before he finally won his first Super Bowl. That was the most of any coach in NFL history.

touchdown passes in a span of four minutes as Kansas City rallied to win 31–20.

THE COMEBACK TRAIL

The Chiefs returned to the Super Bowl a year later only to be thumped by the Tampa Bay Buccaneers 31–9. But that loss did nothing to slow Kansas City's dynasty momentum. Two years later, Mahomes and company were back in the big game against the Philadelphia Eagles.

The two teams put on a thrilling show in Super Bowl LVII. At halftime, Kansas City once again faced a 10-point deficit. The 24–14 scoreline was made worse by the fact that Mahomes had been plagued by an ankle injury suffered two games earlier.

The Chiefs' star gutted it out in another second-half rally. Once again he threw two fourth-quarter touchdown passes to briefly put Kansas City ahead. Mahomes's biggest play, though, came with his legs. With the game tied 35–35 in the final minutes, the quarterback's hobbling 26-yard scramble helped set up a game-winning field goal attempt. Star kicker Harrison Butker drilled a 27-yard attempt with eight seconds left to win the game.

NOT FINISHED

Some NFL observers wondered if the Chiefs still had enough firepower entering the 2023 season. Hill had been traded a few years earlier. Mahomes's receivers entering the year were mostly untested. But the team still had the star quarterback. It also had the larger-than-life Kelce. The tight end's profile had grown through the years due to his playful personality. By the start of the 2023 season, he had hosted *Saturday Night Live* and begun dating pop star Taylor Swift. But despite his growing fame, Kelce was still known in NFL circles as the game's premier, and toughest, tight end.

MVP MAHOMES

Patrick Mahomes was named the Super Bowl MVP in each of the Chiefs' Super Bowl wins. By doing so, he joined Joe Montana as a three-time winner. The 28-year-old Mahomes trailed only Tom Brady, who won the award five times.

The combo led the Chiefs back to the Super Bowl as the other receivers got up to speed. Super Bowl LVIII was a rematch with the 49ers. It did not start well for the defending champions. Kansas City fell behind 10–0 in the second quarter before two Butker field goals made things closer by halftime. The two teams then traded the lead in the third quarter.

With 1:53 left, San Francisco kicker Jake Moody put the 49ers ahead 19–16 on a 53-yard field goal. But with time on the clock, the Chiefs could not be counted out. Mahomes hit five different receivers as he maneuvered his team down the field. His last pass was a 22-yard catch-and-run by Kelce to put the ball at the San Francisco 11-yard line. Butker booted a 29-yard attempt to force overtime.

The Chiefs rush to celebrate after wide receiver Mecole Hardman, *top*, caught a game-winning touchdown pass in overtime of Super Bowl LVIII in February 2024.

San Francisco scored on a field goal on its overtime drive. But the NFL had recently adopted new overtime rules that gave both teams a chance. Once again, Mahomes went to work. He mixed a series of short passes with two scrambles that totaled 27 yards. The Chiefs eventually worked the ball to the 49ers' 3-yard line. On the final play of the first overtime session, Mahomes hit a wide-open Mecole Hardman for the winning score.

For the ninth time in Super Bowl history, a team had won back-to-back championships. But immediately after the game, Mahomes began talking about accomplishing a feat no other NFL team had. "I'm going to do whatever I can to be back in this game next year," he said. "Three-peat."

HONORABLE MENTIONS

MIAMI DOLPHINS

The Dolphins reached three consecutive Super Bowls in the early 1970s under legendary head coach Don Shula. The 1972 squad was the first NFL team to finish a season undefeated. They rounded out a 17–0 campaign by knocking off Washington in Super Bowl VII 14–7. A year later, Miami became the second repeat champions by beating the Minnesota Vikings 24–7 in Super Bowl VIII. Hard-charging running back Larry Csonka led the way with 145 yards and two touchdowns.

DALLAS COWBOYS

Though Dallas lost three Super Bowls in the 1970s, "America's Team" also won twice. The first came in Super Bowl VI in January 1972. That year, the team's vaunted "Doomsday Defense" roughed up the Dolphins in a 24–3 rout. Six years later, the Dallas defense held the Denver Broncos to 156 total yards in Super Bowl XII. That set the stage for a 27–10 romp.

OAKLAND/LOS ANGELES RAIDERS

The Raiders dynasty of the late 1970s and early 1980s spanned two cities. Legendary coach John Madden led the Oakland Raiders to a 32–14 victory over the Minnesota Vikings in Super Bowl XI in January 1977 after years of coming close. The team went back and won Super Bowl XV in January 1981 by knocking off the Philadelphia Eagles 27–10. By the 1983 season, the team had relocated to Los Angeles. But the Raiders took their winning ways to the Southern California city. In Super Bowl XVIII they routed Washington 38–9.

Don Shula

John Elway

NEW YORK GIANTS

Demanding coach Bill Parcells built the Giants up from league laughingstock to powerhouse team in the 1980s. The team finally reached the top after the 1986 season by rocking the Denver Broncos 39–20 in Super Bowl XXI. As the final seconds ticked down, some of the Giants doused Parcells with Gatorade. The celebration soon became a tradition for winning teams in several sports. Four years later, the Giants outlasted the Bills 20–19 in Super Bowl XXV. The game was Parcells's final contest in charge of the Giants. And the team's defense was masterminded by a young coordinator named Bill Belichick.

DENVER BRONCOS

Star quarterback John Elway took the Broncos to three Super Bowls in four years in the late 1980s. Denver was thumped each time. After the 1997 season, the 37-year-old Elway memorably led the team back and beat the Green Bay Packers 31–24 in Super Bowl XXXII. Star running back Terrell Davis scored the winning touchdown with less than two minutes remaining. After the game, team owner Pat Bowlen dedicated the win to Elway. After Denver beat the Atlanta Falcons 34–19 for a repeat title a year later, Bowlen dedicated the second title to the Broncos' fans.

GLOSSARY

blue-collar
Related to manual labor or work.

contenders
Teams that have a good chance at winning a championship.

draft
A system that allows teams to acquire new players coming into a league.

dynasty
A team that has an extended period of success, usually winning multiple championships in the process.

enshrined
Honored by being preserved.

era
A period of time in history.

fluke
An unlikely occurrence.

forfeit
To give up a victory or achievement for breaking a rule.

legacy
Something of importance that came from someone in the past.

merge
To join with another to create something new, such as a company, a team, or a league.

potent
Powerful.

rivalry
A fierce and ongoing competition between two players or teams.

secondary
The defensive players—cornerbacks and safeties—who start the play farthest from the line.

tainted
Spoiled.

underdog
The person or team that is not expected to win.

MORE INFORMATION

Books

Byde, Ben. *Inspiring Football Stories for Kids*. Peregrine, 2024.

Graves, Will. *GOATs of Football*. Abdo, 2022.

Hanlon, Luke. *Football Strategies*. Abdo, 2024.

Online Resources

Booklinks
NONFICTION NETWORK
FREE! ONLINE NONFICTION RESOURCES

To learn more about Super Bowl dynasties, please visit **abdobooklinks.com** or scan this QR code. These links are routinely monitored and updated to provide the most current information available.

INDEX

About the Author

David J. Clarke is a freelance sportswriter. Originally from Helena, Montana, he now lives in Savannah, Georgia.